START HERE

FIND A PENCIL.

TURN TO THE COVER OF THE BOOK. BEGIN DRAWING A LINE IN ANY DIRECTION. TAKE YOUR TIME. THERE IS NO RUSH. BRING THE LINE TO THE BOTTOM EDGE OF THE COVER. CONTINUE THE LINE ONTO THE INSIDE OF THE COVER. COME TO THIS SPOT.

NOW, MOVE THE LINE DOWN THE PAGE.

CIRCLE THE TITLE WITH THE LINE.

WRITE YOUR NAME.

CONTINUE THE LINE DOWN THE PAGE.

THE LINE

KERI SMITH

PENGUIN BOOKS

MOVE LINE DOWN AND ONTO THE NEXT PAGE. ⌄⌄⌄

CONTINUE THE LINE DOWN THE
COPYRIGHT PAGE. MAKE A FEW
SCRIBBLES HERE AND THERE.
DRAW OVER THE COPYRIGHT TEXT,
CIRCLE SOME NUMBERS, CIRCLE
SOME WORDS JUST FOR THE HELL
OF IT.

PENGUIN BOOKS

An imprint of Penguin Random House LLC
375 Hudson Street
New York, New York 10014
penguin.com

ISBN 9780143108467

Printed in the United States of America
1   3   5   7   9   10   8   6   4   2

V

THE BEGINNING

ARE YOU HERE? YES?

OK, GOOD.

YOU HAVE STARTED A JOURNEY.
THIS LINE WILL BE YOUR COMPANION,
LIKE A THIN THREAD THAT LEADS YOU
THROUGH A MAZE.

IT MIGHT GET MESSY OR CONFUSING
AT TIMES. IN FACT, I CAN GUARANTEE
IT WILL BE CHALLENGING. TRUST THAT
ALL WILL BE ILLUMINATED IN THE END.

ALL THAT EXISTS IS YOU AND THIS PENCIL.

DO NOT LEAVE THE LINE AND TRY TO
START SOMEWHERE ELSE OR
YOU WILL BE LOST!
DO NOT LOOK AHEAD!

MOVE LINE DOWN AND ONTO THE NEXT PAGE. ⌄ ⌄

YOU CAN TAKE A BREAK AT ANY TIME. WHEN YOU ARE READY TO BEGIN AGAIN, CONTINUE EXACTLY WHERE YOU LEFT OFF.

YOU MIGHT BE THINKING, "BUT I DON'T KNOW WHERE THE LINE IS HEADED OR WHAT WILL BE ASKED OF ME! WHAT IF IT TAKES ME SOMEWHERE I DON'T WANT TO GO?" THAT IS ENTIRELY POSSIBLE. BUT YOUR JOB RIGHT NOW IS TO FOCUS ON THE TIP OF YOUR PENCIL.

ARE YOU WILLING TO GO ON AN ADVENTURE WITHOUT KNOWING WHERE YOU WILL GO?

MOVE LINE DOWN AND ONTO THE NEXT PAGE. ⌄⌄⌄

BUT WHAT IS THE LINE?

AN ADVENTURE, AN EXPERIMENT, A TEST,
A FIGMENT, A PHILOSOPHY, A CLUB,
A DREAM, A SYMBOL, A MOVEMENT,
A STATE OF MIND, A TRANSFORMATION,
A QUEST, A DARE, A DIVERSION,
AN EXPLORATION, A CHALLENGE.

IT MIGHT BE ALL OF THESE THINGS.
OR IT COULD BE NONE. YOU HAVE
TO EXPERIENCE IT TO FIND OUT.
IT IS DIFFERENT FOR EVERY PERSON.

GO TO THE GUTTER HERE.

gut·ter \ˈgə-tər\ noun:
THE BLANK SPACE BETWEEN
FACING PAGES OF A BOOK.

EXPLORE THE GUTTER WITH THE
PENCIL. LEAVE SOMETHING SMALL
IN THE GUTTER.

MOVE LINE DOWN AND ONTO THE NEXT PAGE. ⌄⌄⌄

A FEW INSTRUCTIONS

IF YOU ARE NOT ABLE TO WRITE
IN CURSIVE, THEN CONTINUE THE
LINE AT THE END OF YOUR
WRITINGS.

ALWAYS PICK UP THE LINE ON THE
NEXT PAGE CLOSE TO WHERE YOU
LEFT OFF ON THE PREVIOUS PAGE.
IT SHOULD FLOW EASILY FROM PAGE
TO PAGE.

DO NOT STOP OR DISCONNECT THE
LINE UNLESS INSTRUCTED TO.

LET THE LINE VENTURE TO TOUCH
EACH EDGE OF THIS PAGE.

MOVE LINE DOWN AND ONTO THE NEXT PAGE. ∨∨∨

MOVE THE PENCIL

FAST AND SLOW

WITHOUT LIFTING IT FROM THE PAGE.

LISTEN TO THE SOUND IT IS
MAKING.

MOVE LINE DOWN AND ONTO THE NEXT PAGE. ⌄⌄⌄

YOU'RE STILL GETTING WARMED
UP. LET'S LOOSEN UP SOME MORE.
HOW ABOUT MAKING SOME LARGE
CIRCLES OR SWIRLING MOTIONS?

RELAX YOUR WRIST.

DON'T THINK—
JUST MOVE THE PENCIL.

MOVE LINE DOWN AND ONTO THE NEXT PAGE. ⌄
⌄
⌄

TRAVEL NOW TO THE
PRECIPICE, THE EDGE.
JUMP OFF. GO
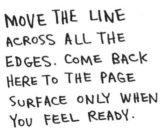
OVER THE EDGE. >
MOVE THE LINE
ACROSS ALL THE
EDGES. COME BACK
HERE TO THE PAGE
SURFACE ONLY WHEN
YOU FEEL READY.

REPEAT.

REPEAT.

REPEAT.

HOW DO YOU FEEL SO FAR?
(CIRCLE ONE)

A) INTRIGUED
B) COMMITTED
C) UNSURE
D) DONE

IF YOU ANSWERED A OR B, THE LINE IS BECOMING PART OF YOU. A VEHICLE FOR A NEW EXPERIENCE. YOUR MARK. PROOF THAT YOU WERE HERE. YOUR DRAWING ON THE WORLD. THE SECRET THAT YOU HAVE BEEN PURSUING. PLEASE MOVE ON TO THE NEXT PAGE.

IF YOU ANSWERED C, PLEASE MOVE ON TO THE NEXT PAGE. TRY A FEW MORE PAGES JUST TO SEE. SOMETIMES DISCOMFORT IS GOOD, NON?

IF YOU ANSWERED D, IT'S OK TO QUIT. GIVE THE BOOK AWAY. CLOSE IT UP AND PUT IT IN A DRAWER FOR GOOD. IT IS NO LONGER YOURS. GOOD-BYE. BEST WISHES.

ARE YOU STILL HERE? YOU COULDN'T DO
IT, COULD YOU?

WHAT IF YOU WERE MISSING OUT ON
SOMETHING, SOMETHING THAT OTHER
PEOPLE WERE FINDING AND THAT YOU
MIGHT FIND TOO, SOMETHING ABOUT
YOURSELF?

WHAT IF THE LINE IS HOLDING A

SECRET?

THE LINE IS CAPABLE OF ANYTHING.
MAYBE IT CONTAINS A POWERFUL ENERGY.

BRING THE LINE TO THE CENTER
OF THE PAGE AND DRAW A
LARGE SCRIBBLE. GO REALLY
FAST. AS FAST AS YOU CAN.
FASTER.

SEE WHAT I MEAN? THERE IS
SOMETHING TO IT. SOMETHING INTERESTING.
BUT WHAT?
I THINK YOU HAVE NO CHOICE BUT
TO CONTINUE.

MOVE LINE DOWN AND ONTO THE NEXT PAGE. ⌄⌄

THE ENERGY IN THE LINE IS
GROWING. IT SEEMS TO WANT
TO BURST OFF THE PAGE AND
LEAP OUT INTO THE WORLD.

DRAW AN EVEN LARGER
SCRIBBLE.

MOVE LINE DOWN AND ONTO THE NEXT PAGE.

^
^ ^
^

THE LINE CAN BE MEDITATIVE.
LET IT FLOW, WANDER,
MEANDER, DRIFT.
MOVE IT FROM ONE SIDE TO THE OTHER;
REPEAT UNTIL THE PAGE IS FULL.
IT IS FREE.

MOVE LINE DOWN AND ONTO THE NEXT PAGE. ˅ ˅

STOP.

REST.

RIGHT HERE.

TAKE A DEEP BREATH.

THIS MOMENT IS ALL WE HAVE.

LET ALL THOUGHTS GO.

WE DON'T NEED THEM RIGHT NOW.

CONTEMPLATE ONLY YOU AND THE LINE.

SIT FOR A MOMENT.

MOVE LINE DOWN AND ONTO THE NEXT PAGE. ⌄⌄⌄

ʌ
ʌ ʌ
 ʌ

LET'S TRY SOMETHING NEW,
SHALL WE? TAPE THE PENCIL
TO YOUR FOOT SOMEHOW AND
MOVE THE LINE AROUND ON
THE PAGE USING YOUR LEG.
IT PROBABLY FEELS A BIT AWKWARD,
DOESN'T IT? SOME THINGS ARE
LIKE THAT. TRY IT WITH YOUR
EYES CLOSED.

MOVE LINE DOWN AND ONTO THE NEXT PAGE. ∨∨∨

FORM A BUNCH OF
RANDOM FOLDS
AT THE BOTTOM OF THE PAGE.
CONTINUE THE LINE OVER THE
FOLDS AND BACK UP HERE AGAIN.
UNFOLD. WHAT HAPPENED?

FORM RANDOM
FOLDS HERE

MOVE LINE DOWN AND ONTO THE NEXT PAGE. ⌄⌄⌄

^
^ ^
^

OH NO!

THE LINE IS FRAGMENTED.

TRY TO JOIN THE LINE UP SO IT
IS WHOLE AGAIN.

WHEW! THANK GOODNESS.

MOVE LINE DOWN AND ONTO THE NEXT PAGE. ∨∨∨

DOES THE LINE EXIST AT ALL?
OR IS IT A FIGMENT OF YOUR
IMAGINATION? WHAT IF THE LINE
IS A TRAP, CAUSING YOU TO SPEND
YOUR DAYS WASTING TIME DOING
NOTHING? IF THAT'S TRUE, YOU
MIGHT FEEL RESENTMENT
TOWARD IT. THERE ARE MUCH
BETTER THINGS YOU COULD BE
DOING. HOW CAN YOU FREE
YOURSELF FROM IT?

TURN THE LINE INTO SOME KIND OF
ENCLOSURE HERE.

MOVE LINE DOWN AND ONTO THE NEXT PAGE. ∨∨∨

⌃
⌃ ⌃

I THINK YOU MAY HAVE OFFENDED
THE LINE. IT'S REQUESTING SOME
ALONE TIME.

COVER IT UP
WITH SOMETHING OF YOUR CHOOSING

(YOU CAN SEW, GLUE, TAPE, PAINT).

MOVE LINE DOWN AND ONTO THE NEXT PAGE. ⌄⌄⌄

THE LINE IS FEELING A LITTLE
MISCHIEVOUS AFTER THAT LAST
PAGE.
USE THE LINE TO DEFACE
THIS IMAGE.
BOTH YOU AND THE LINE WILL
FEEL MUCH BETTER AFTERWARD —
TRUST ME.

MOVE LINE DOWN AND ONTO THE NEXT PAGE. <small>ⱽ</small>
<small>ⱽ</small>

THE ENERGY OF THE LINE HAS BECOME
VERY SMALL.

MAKE INCREDIBLY TINY
MOTIONS AND SHAPES
WITH THE LINE.

MOVE LINE DOWN AND ONTO THE NEXT PAGE. ∨∨∨

IT'S ABOUT TO GET MORE INTERESTING.
(DO YOU FEEL YOUR EXCITEMENT
BUILDING?)

WE ARE GOING TO DELVE INTO YOUR
HEAD A LITTLE. THE LINE IS GOING
TO DEMONSTRATE YOUR CURRENT MOOD.
SHOW HOW YOU ARE FEELING
USING THE LINE. LET IT MOVE IN
WHATEVER WAY FEELS MOST NATURAL
TO YOU RIGHT NOW.

MOVE LINE DOWN AND ONTO THE NEXT PAGE. ⌄⌄⌄

THE LINE DISAPPEARS INTO THIS
HOLE. OR DOES IT? MAYBE IT
PROCEEDS SAFELY AROUND IT
INSTEAD?

KNOW THAT YOU WILL BE OK
EITHER WAY. HOLES CAN BE
PLENTIFUL AND DON'T
NECESSARILY NEED TO BE
AVOIDED. PROCEED AS YOU SEE
FIT.

MOVE LINE DOWN AND ONTO THE NEXT PAGE. ⌄⌄⌄

USE THE LINE TO CREATE

A GIANT MAZE.

IS THE LINE LOST OR IS IT HIDING?

MOVE LINE DOWN AND ONTO THE NEXT PAGE. ⌄⌄⌄

THERE ARE TIMES WHEN THINGS GET
BUMPY. PLACE THIS PAGE OVER
SOME PAVEMENT.
CONTINUE THE LINE. THE LINE WILL
MOVE IN UNPREDICTABLE WAYS. YOU
WILL NOT BE ABLE TO KEEP IT
STRAIGHT. BUT KEEP TRYING TO
MAKE THE LINE STRAIGHT ANYWAY.
OR WHAT IF YOU JUST ACCEPT THE
BUMPS — MOVE WITH THEM, SO TO
SPEAK?

MOVE LINE DOWN AND ONTO THE NEXT PAGE.

YOU ARE GOING TO HAVE TO CUT THE LINE.

YES, IT'S TRUE.

CONTINUE THE LINE DOWN THE PAGE
AND THEN

CUT THE PAGE
IN HALF.

IT IS POSSIBLE TO REATTACH IT. SOMEHOW.

CONTINUE THE LINE ONTO THE NEXT PAGE ANY
WAY YOU CAN.

THE LINE IS NOW GOING TO ATTEMPT
TO COVER EVERY INCH OF THIS PAGE.

EVERY INCH.

WHEN YOU ARE READY TO MOVE ON TO
THE NEXT PAGE, YOU WILL KNOW.
YOUR INTUITION WILL TELL YOU, GETTING
STRONGER THE MORE YOU TRUST IN IT.
THE FUTURE OF THE LINE WILL DEPEND
ON YOU TRUSTING IT.

MOVE LINE DOWN AND ONTO THE NEXT PAGE. ˅ ˅ ˅

^
^ ^
^

THE LINE WANTS TO TAKE OVER. LET IT. SOMETIMES IT'S HELPFUL TO TAKE A STEP BACK AND RELINQUISH CONTROL COMPLETELY.

MOVE LINE DOWN AND ONTO THE NEXT PAGE. ⌄ ⌄ ⌄

^
^
^

THE LINE HAS BEEN INFUSED WITH ELECTRIC ⌇ ENERGY.

LET IT EXPLODE!

MOVE LINE DOWN AND ONTO THE NEXT PAGE. ˅˅˅

^
^
^

THE LINE WILL NOW BECOME
A FORM OF MEDITATION.

DRAW A SLOW,
REPETITIVE
PATTERN
COVERING THIS ENTIRE PAGE.

MOVE LINE DOWN AND ONTO THE NEXT PAGE. ⌄⌄⌄

IT IS QUITE POSSIBLE THAT THE LINE IS A MICROCOSM OF THE UNIVERSE. USING THE LINE, DRAW A MANDALA (A CIRCULAR, GEOMETRIC PATTERN).

MOVE LINE DOWN AND ONTO THE NEXT PAGE.

^
^
^

THE LINE HAS BECOME A PART OF
THE <u>HISTORY</u> <u>OF ALL THINGS</u>
FROM THE BEGINNING OF TIME,
AND IT HAS THIN THREADS CONNECTING
IT TO EVERYTHING. IT HAS BECOME ITS
OWN STORY. DOES IT HAVE A
BEGINNING OR AN END?
DRAW THE THREADS
COMING OFF OF IT, CONNECTING
IT TO EVERYTHING.

MOVE LINE DOWN AND ONTO THE NEXT PAGE. ⌄⌄

THE LINE IS TRANSFORMING INTO A

REFUGE

FOR ITS USER.

DO YOU FEEL IT? DRAW A SAFE
PLACE USING THE LINE.

MOVE LINE DOWN AND ONTO THE NEXT PAGE. ⌄⌄⌄

⌄
⌄
⌄

THE LINE IS NOW ENTERING AN
ALTERNATE REALITY WHERE NOTHING
IS AS IT WAS. IT'S BECOMING
BLURRED TO THE POINT THAT YOU CAN
HARDLY SEE IT. DO SOMETHING TO
BLUR IT FURTHER.

MOVE LINE DOWN AND ONTO THE NEXT PAGE. ⌄
⌄
⌄

THE LINE WINDS AROUND ITSELF
TO CREATE A

BIG BALL OF
STRING,

LIKE A GIANT KNOT THAT CAN
NEVER BE UNTANGLED.

MOVE LINE DOWN AND ONTO THE NEXT PAGE. ⌄⌄⌄

THE LINE IS BECOMING UNPREDICTABLE.
ITS PATH ALTERED USING CHANCE
VARIABLES.

1 = SCRIBBLES
2 = BUMPS
3 = GRID
4 = GO TO THE NEXT PAGE
5 = FAST
6 = DON'T MOVE FOR FIVE MINUTES

ROLL A DIE.

MOVE LINE DOWN AND ONTO THE NEXT PAGE. ⌄⌄⌄

THE POWER OF THE LINE IS GROWING.

DO YOU FEEL IT?

OVER THE NEXT FEW PAGES YOU ARE
GOING TO BE ASKED TO DO SOMETHING
TERRIFYING. ARE YOU READY TO ACCEPT
THE CHALLENGE? IS YOUR IMAGINATION
RUNNING WILD?

WHAT COULD IT BE?

PONDER THE POSSIBILITIES WHILE YOU
PROCRASTINATE TURNING THE PAGE BY

DOODLING
AIMLESSLY

HERE. (SOMETIMES AVOIDANCE OF
SOMETHING SCARY IS PERFECTLY
ACCEPTABLE.)

MOVE LINE DOWN AND ONTO THE NEXT PAGE.

You ARE NOW GOING TO

TURN TO THE NEXT PAGE.

(DO YOU FEEL A BIT GIDDY RIGHT NOW?)

THIS BOOK IS NOT FOR THE FAINT OF HEART; YOU, DEAR READER, SHOULD KNOW THAT BY NOW. YOU HAVE NO ONE TO BLAME BUT YOURSELF.

MOVE LINE DOWN AND ONTO THE NEXT PAGE. ∨∨∨

LEAVE THE LINE FOR A MOMENT.
(I KNOW I SAID TO NEVER LEAVE
THE LINE, BUT IN THIS INSTANCE IT
IS OK; IT'S JUST FOR A MOMENT.)

IN THE MIDDLE OF THE CIRCLE WRITE
DOWN ONE OF YOUR

GREATEST FEARS.

CONTINUE THE LINE OVER TO THE
CIRCLE. CONTEMPLATE THE FEAR.
CONFRONT IT HEAD-ON.
LOOK AT IT.

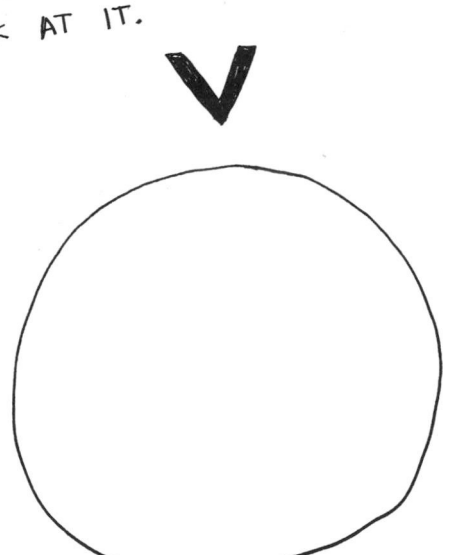

TAKE A DEEP BREATH.

MOVE LINE DOWN AND ONTO THE NEXT PAGE. ∨∨∨

THAT MIGHT HAVE BEEN A BIT ROUGH,
BUT YOU ARE OK. YOU COULD PROBABLY
USE A DIVERSION RIGHT ABOUT NOW.

LET'S TRY THIS:

TAKE THE PAGE BELOW AND ROLL IT
INTO A TUBE TOWARD THE GUTTER.

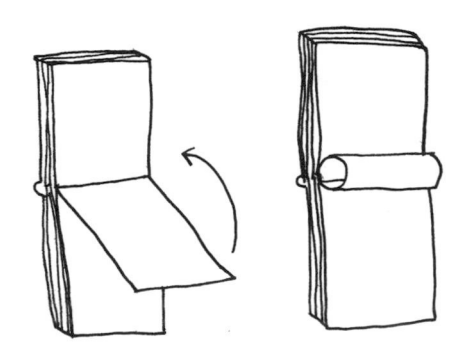

MOVE THE LINE DOWN AND OVER THE BUMP.
FOLLOW THE DIRECTIONS ON THE NEXT PAGE.

MOVE LINE DOWN AND ONTO THE NEXT PAGE. ∨
∨
∨

HELLO. I THINK YOU SHOULD GO
BACK OVER THE
BUMP, THEN COME BACK DOWN
HERE AGAIN.

MOVE LINE DOWN AND ONTO THE NEXT PAGE. ∨∨∨

ARE YOU THINKING OF OTHER PLACES YOU WOULD RATHER BE? FOCUS ON THE LINE. IF YOUR MIND DRIFTS, BRING IT BACK TO THE LINE. IF THOUGHTS COME IN, LABEL THEM AS "THOUGHTS" AND BRING YOUR ATTENTION BACK TO THE LINE. BREATHE. CONTINUE THE LINE WHEN YOU ARE READY.

MOVE LINE DOWN AND ONTO THE NEXT PAGE.

∨
∨
∨

ARE YOU FINDING YOURSELF BECOMING
A LITTLE ATTACHED TO THE LINE?
YOU HAVE A BIT OF HISTORY TOGETHER
NOW. MAYBE YOU'D LIKE TO TAKE
A JOURNEY. ANOTHER DIVERSION.

RUN UP AND DOWN THESE HILLS.

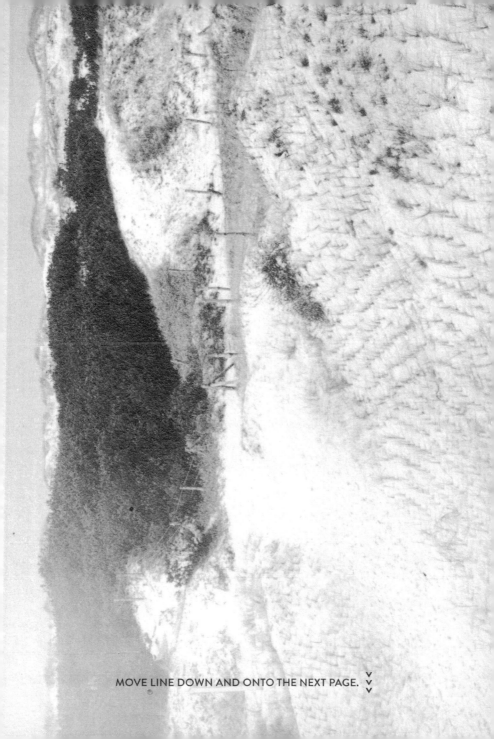

MOVE LINE DOWN AND ONTO THE NEXT PAGE. ⌄⌄⌄

v
v
v

OH DEAR. SOME BUSY TERRAIN
UP AHEAD. YOU WILL NEED SOME
NAVIGATION SKILLS.

FIND A PATH

DOWN TO THE BOTTOM OF THE
PAGE.

PROCEED CAUTIOUSLY.

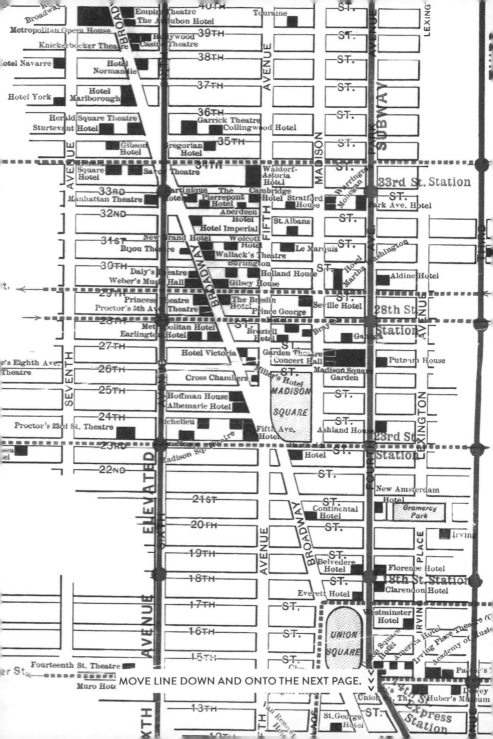

MOVE LINE DOWN AND ONTO THE NEXT PAGE.

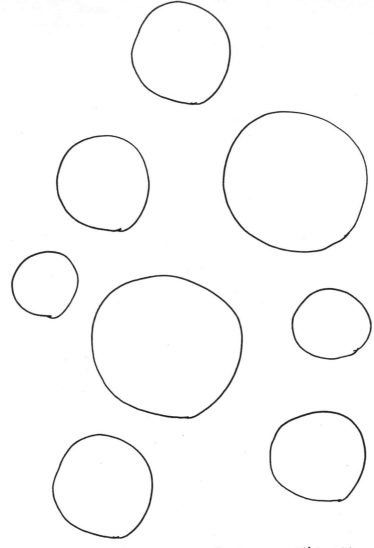

WRITE A LIST
OF THINGS YOU ARE AVOIDING
IN THESE CIRCLES.

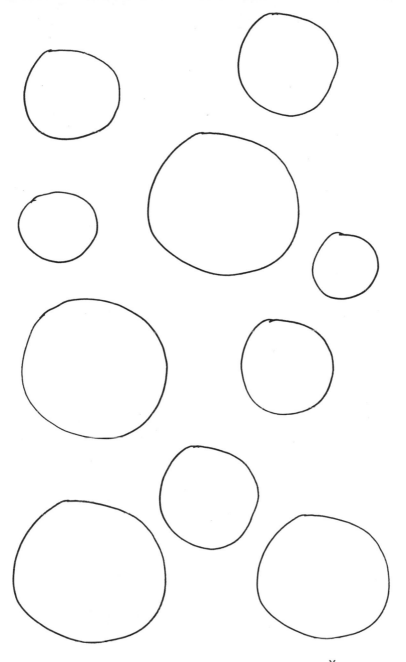

MOVE LINE DOWN AND ONTO THE NEXT PAGE. ⌄⌄⌄

THIS NEXT EVENT IS GOING
TO BE COOL.

BRING THE LINE DOWN HERE.

WRAP THE LINE

AROUND THE BACK OF THE BOOK
SEVERAL TIMES.

EXIT HERE   RETURN HERE

MOVE LINE DOWN AND ONTO THE NEXT PAGE. ⌄⌄⌄

THAT WAS GOOD, BUT LET'S GO FURTHER.
MAYBE IT WOULD BE BEST TO TAKE THIS
ONE OUTSIDE.

BRING THE LINE
OUTSIDE OF THE BOOK.
LET IT CIRCLE YOU COMPLETELY.

EXIT HERE   RETURN HERE

SOMETIMES THINGS GET VERY MESSY.
DROP SOME SUBSTANCES HERE.

DRAG THE LINE

THROUGH THEM.

MOVE LINE DOWN AND ONTO THE NEXT PAGE. ∨∨

(IS IT TIME FOR SHARPENING YET? LOCATE A SHARPENER.

TEST YOUR LINE.

SOMETIMES A LITTLE SHARPENING OR FINE-TUNING GIVES US A NEW OUTLOOK.)

NOW THAT YOU HAVE A SHARPENER,
WHY DON'T YOU BREAK THE TIP
OF THE PENCIL ON PURPOSE WHILE
YOU ARE DRAWING? GO AHEAD. SEE
WHAT HAPPENS. DO IT SEVERAL
TIMES. DO YOU FIND IT FRUSTRATING?
PERHAPS IT COULD BE LIBERATING.

MOVE LINE DOWN AND ONTO THE NEXT PAGE. ∨∨∨

^
^ ^
^

SOMETIMES WE JUST NEED A
LITTLE LIGHTHEARTEDNESS. LET
YOUR LINE GET
            LIGHTER.
LET IT ALMOST FADE COMPLETELY.
PLAY WITH THAT LIGHT LINE.
LET IT INFUSE YOU WITH ITS CALMNESS.

LET THE LINE BE A REFUGE OF QUIET
FOR YOU.

MOVE LINE DOWN AND ONTO THE NEXT PAGE. ˅˅˅

WHAT IF THE LINE BECAME
A TACTILE EXPERIENCE?

PLACE THE TIPS OF YOUR FINGERS HERE.

TRACE YOUR FINGERS
SLOWLY WITH THE LINE.

MOVE LINE DOWN AND ONTO THE NEXT PAGE. ˅
˅
˅

^
^
^
^

BRING THE LINE
ONTO YOUR
BODY
(YOU MAY HAVE TO
SWITCH TO PEN*),
AND CARRY IT WITH
YOU AS YOU GO
ABOUT YOUR DAY.
GIVE IT SOME
PERSONAL MEANING
(FOR EXAMPLE, "THE
LINE IS A REMINDER
TO BREATHE").

* MAKE SURE THE PEN
  IS NONTOXIC.

MOVE LINE DOWN AND ONTO THE NEXT PAGE.

WHAT IF THE PATH OF YOUR LIFE
WERE ALTERED JUST BECAUSE YOU WENT IN
ONE DIRECTION
INSTEAD OF ANOTHER? WHAT IF
LITTLE DECISIONS CHANGED YOUR
COURSE?

SEND THE LINE
THIS WAY

OR

SEND THE LINE
THIS WAY

^
^
^

SOMETIMES THE LINE WANTS TO TRAVEL IN CIRCLES. OTHER TIMES IT WANTS TO UNWIND.

CIRCLE IN, THEN

CIRCLE OUT —

AND INTO ANOTHER CIRCLE.

MOVE LINE DOWN AND ONTO THE NEXT PAGE. ⌄⌄⌄

^
^
^

THE LINE COULD USE SOME DIVERSITY
IN ITS EXPERIENCES.

GLUE SOME THINGS

HERE THAT YOU WOULD LIKE THE LINE TO
INTERACT WITH. ALLOW THEM TO MEET UP.

HOW MIGHT YOUR LINE INTERACT
WITH SOMEONE ELSE'S LINE?

MOVE LINE DOWN AND ONTO THE NEXT PAGE. ⌄⌄

WHAT IF THE LINE BECAME A CRACK
IN YOUR FOUNDATION, REPRESENTING
A CHANGE,

A NEW PATH,

A DIVERSION FROM YOUR PREVIOUS WAY
OF BEING? LET IT BECOME THE NEW PATH.

WHAT WOULD YOU LIKE TO CHANGE?
USE THE LINE TO LAY OUT SOME NEW
DIRECTIONS FOR YOUR FUTURE.

WHERE DO YOU WANT TO GO?

WHERE DO YOU WANT TO PUT THE
ENERGY OF YOUR LINE?

MOVE LINE DOWN AND ONTO THE NEXT PAGE. ⌄ ⌄ ⌄

v v v

OCCASIONALLY THINGS CAN BECOME
A BIT TEDIOUS. BUT THE LINE
PERSISTS.

TRAVEL THROUGH
EACH SQUARE — TWICE.

BUT NOT IN A STRAIGHT LINE.

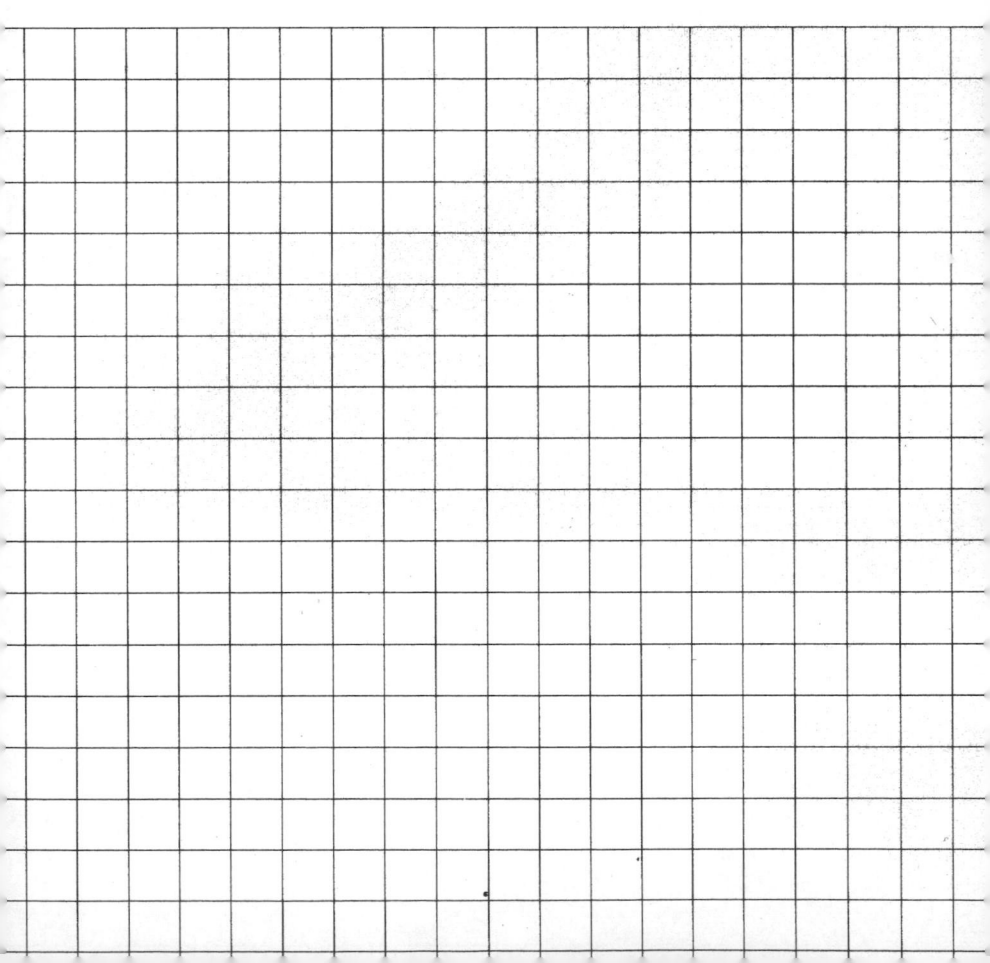

MOVE LINE DOWN AND ONTO THE NEXT PAGE. ∨
∨
∨

WHEW. THANK GOODNESS THAT IS OVER.

EXCEPT... YOU CAN ALSO GET STUCK
GOING AROUND IN CIRCLES.

GO AROUND

THE OBSTRUCTION ONE HUNDRED TIMES.

YOU ARE FREE AGAIN.

MOVE LINE DOWN AND ONTO THE NEXT PAGE. ⌄⌄⌄

^
^ ^
^

DID THE LAST PAGE FRUSTRATE YOU?
ARE YOU FEELING IMPATIENT?
ARE YOU WONDERING YET AGAIN
WHAT THE POINT OF ALL THIS IS?

IN MOST BOOKS, THIS IS USUALLY
WHEN THE PLOT TAKES A SUDDEN
AND DRAMATIC SHIFT.

WAIT FOR IT.

CONTEMPLATE THE POSSIBILITIES.

CONTINUE.

MOVE LINE DOWN AND ONTO THE NEXT PAGE. ∨∨∨

^
^ ^
^

GO TO SOMEONE YOU TRUST.

GIVE THEM CONTROL

OVER THE LINE FOR THE NEXT
FEW PAGES.
GOOD LUCK.

NOTE TO THE PERSON TAKING OVER
THE LINE:

THANK YOU FOR AGREEING TO DO THIS.
YOU ARE GOING TO HAVE A LITTLE
ADVENTURE. BUT DON'T WORRY —
YOU DON'T HAVE TO SHARE
WHAT GOES ON HERE. IT WILL
BE OUR LITTLE SECRET.

BEGINNING ON THE NEXT PAGE,
DOODLE MINDLESSLY FOR ABOUT
TEN MINUTES.

CONTINUE THE LINE FROM
WHERE THE OWNER OF THIS
BOOK LEFT OFF AND ON TO
THE NEXT PAGE.

MOVE LINE DOWN AND ONTO THE NEXT PAGE. ∨∨∨

OK, ARE YOU FINISHED?

NOW GLUE OR TAPE

THIS PAGE TO THE PREVIOUS PAGE.

GIVE THE LINE BACK TO ITS
OWNER.

MOVE LINE DOWN AND ONTO THE NEXT PAGE. ∨∨∨

OH, HI. IT'S YOU AGAIN. ARE YOU CURIOUS ABOUT WHAT YOU MISSED?

HOW DID YOU FEEL?

A) EXCITED/GIDDY

B) UNSURE/HESITANT

C) COMPLETELY CONFIDENT — NO RESERVATIONS

D) SAD — YOU MISSED THE LINE

YOU WILL JUST HAVE TO ACCEPT THE FACT THAT YOU WILL NEVER, EVER KNOW WHAT WENT ON HERE.

MOVE LINE DOWN AND ONTO THE NEXT PAGE.

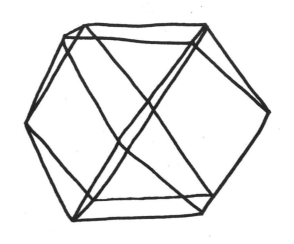

RE-CREATE THIS SHAPE WITH THE LINE.

STARE AT THE SHAPE.

TASK:
YOU MUST COMPLETE THE FOLLOWING
IN ORDER FOR YOU TO MOVE AHEAD

COMFORTABLE CHALLENGES ARISE.
SOMETIMES WHEN YOU ARE FEELING

^
^
^

MOVE LINE DOWN AND ONTO THE NEXT PAGE. ⌄⌄⌄

WHAT IF THE LINE TOOK ON A LIFE OF ITS OWN? WHAT IF THE LINE ESCAPED? MAYBE IT DOES THINGS WHILE YOU SLEEP THAT YOU DON'T KNOW ABOUT...

THE LINE HAS DEFINITELY TAKEN ON A PERSONA. IT CAN MIMIC A FACE.

CIRCLE AROUD THE DOTS AND SEE WHAT APPEARS.

MOVE LINE DOWN AND ONTO THE NEXT PAGE. ⌄⌄⌄

IF YOU HAVEN'T ALREADY, YOU
WILL NOW START TO NOTICE

LINES MADE BY
OTHERS EVERYWHERE

YOU GO.

USING YOUR LINE, COPY SOME OF
THEM HERE. WHAT DO YOU SEE?

MOVE LINE DOWN AND ONTO THE NEXT PAGE.

I KNOW YOU STILL HAVE QUESTIONS.
WHAT IS THE MEANING OF THE LINE?
WHY ARE YOU STILL DRAWING IT?

WHAT IS THE POINT?

THESE ARE IMPORTANT QUESTIONS.
THE ANSWERS ARE CONTAINED IN
THE LINE ITSELF. THE LINE MAY
REVEAL THEM TO YOU, BUT ONLY
IF YOU ARE READY TO HEAR THEM.
FOR NOW WE MUST STILL EXIST IN
THE REALM OF MYSTERY. WHAT IS
THE LINE TRYING TO TELL YOU?
PONDER THE ANSWER BELOW.

MOVE LINE DOWN AND ONTO THE NEXT PAGE. ˅ ˅ ˅

THINK FOR A MOMENT ABOUT ALL THE
LINES IN YOUR LIFE. LINES YOU HAVE
MADE. LINES MADE BY OTHERS.

SIMPLE LINES. COMPLEX LINES.
LINES ACROSS HISTORY. MARKS
MADE WITH ALL MANNER OF
UTENSILS, WITH ANCIENT INKS,
CHARCOAL, BALLPOINT PENS.

HUMANS WILL DO ANYTHING TO
LEAVE THEIR MARK. (YOU WILL
NOW BE SOMEWHAT OBSESSED
WITH LINES EVERYWHERE YOU
GO.)

CONTINUE THE LINE USING

DIFFERENT
UTENSILS

HERE.

TRANSFORM THE LINE INTO

ANOTHER

MEDIUM

(ROCKS, TAPE, STRING),

AND ALLOW IT TO GO TO PLACES
IT HASN'T BEEN BEFORE (TREES,
WALLS, GREAT HEIGHTS — COULD
THE LINE FLY?).

MOVE LINE DOWN AND ONTO THE NEXT PAGE. ⌄⌄⌄

NOW THAT YOU KNOW THE LINE
CONTAINS ITS OWN SECRETS,
USE IT TO WRITE

A SECRET OF
YOUR OWN.

MOVE LINE DOWN AND ONTO THE NEXT PAGE. v v v

THIS IS A SMALL, RANDOM ADVENTURE
IN THE MIDST OF A LARGER ONE.

NO ONE KNOWS THE RESULTS. NOT YET
ANYWAY.

CLOSE YOUR
EYES.

DRAW OR WRITE SOMETHING THAT
YOU WOULD LIKE TO REMEMBER
FOREVER. WHEN YOU ARE DONE
OPEN YOUR EYES.

MOVE LINE DOWN AND ONTO THE NEXT PAGE. ∨∨∨

WHAT IF YOU CANNOT GO BACK TO
WHO YOU WERE BEFORE THE LINE?
WHAT IF, BY DRAWING YOUR LINE,
RIGHT NOW, YOU ARE CREATING AND
PARTICIPATING IN THE STORY OF
YOUR LIFE? WHAT IF THE LINE IS
AN INTEGRAL PART OF THE PERSON
YOU ARE BECOMING? WHAT IF YOU
AND THE LINE ARE MERGING?

ON THIS PAGE

TRACK THE PATH OF YOUR DAY.

KNOW THAT THIS DAY WILL NEVER
BE REPEATED.

MOVE LINE DOWN AND ONTO THE NEXT PAGE.

USE THE LINE TO WRITE SOME OF YOUR

CURRENT THOUGHTS

HERE.

YOU HAVE PERMISSION TO BE FRIGHTFULLY
HONEST.

∨
∨
∨

MOVE LINE DOWN AND ONTO THE NEXT PAGE. ∨
∨

(THE LINE IS NOW ABLE TO ACCESS YOUR
INTUITION WHENEVER IT NEEDS TO.
YOU JUST NEED TO GIVE IT PERMISSION.)

WHAT WOULD YOU LIKE TO INVESTIGATE?
(SOME OF THE MEANING OF YOUR LIFE
WILL NOW EMERGE BELOW.)

CURIOSITY IS WHAT KEEPS YOU GOING,
IS IT NOT? WHAT IS LIFE WITHOUT IT?
WHAT IS THE LINE WITHOUT IT?

USE THE LINE TO WRITE A
LIST OF THINGS YOU
ARE CURIOUS ABOUT.

MOVE LINE DOWN AND ONTO THE NEXT PAGE. ⌄⌄⌄

WHAT IS THE MOST DARING THING YOU'VE EVER WRITTEN OR THOUGHT? THE LINE IS FEELING DARING RIGHT ABOUT NOW.

MOVE LINE DOWN AND ONTO THE NEXT PAGE. ⌄⌄⌄

WHILE WE'RE BEING HONEST, WRITE
A LIST OF THINGS THAT MAKE YOU
ANGRY.

MOVE LINE DOWN AND ONTO THE NEXT PAGE. ∨∨∨

˄
˄
˄

MAKE A STATEMENT

USING THE LINE (SOMETHING YOU'VE BEEN WANTING TO SAY BUT HAVE BEEN AFRAID TO). IT COULD ALSO BE A VOW TO YOURSELF TO DO SOMETHING DIFFERENTLY.

MOVE LINE DOWN AND ONTO THE NEXT PAGE. ∨∨∨

ALLOW THE LINE TO REFLECT THIS
CURRENT MOMENT
IN ANY WAY THAT FEELS RIGHT.

MOVE LINE DOWN AND ONTO THE NEXT PAGE. ⌄⌄⌄

IT'S GETTING SOMEWHAT HEAVY IN HERE.
MAYBE TIME TO LIGHTEN UP A LITTLE?
LET'S PARTAKE IN THIS
OBSTACLE COURSE
FOR A BIT. LET THE LINE INTERACT
WITH THESE SHAPES.

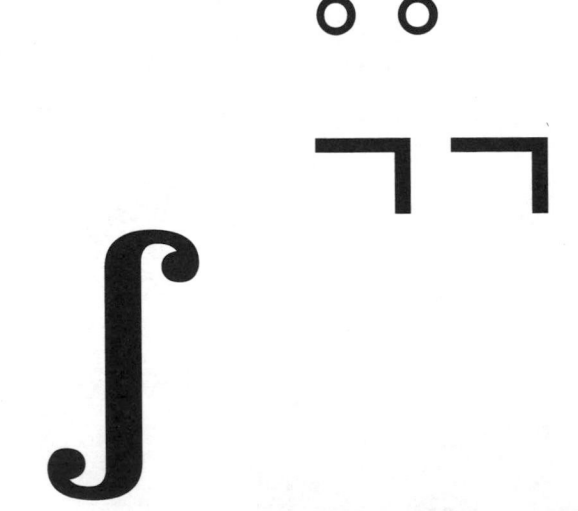

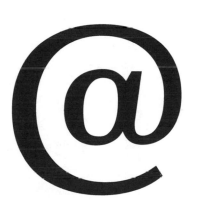

MOVE LINE DOWN AND ONTO THE NEXT PAGE.

WHEW. TIME TO REST.

LET THE LINE DRIFT;

TURN IT INTO

WATER.

MOVE LINE DOWN AND ONTO THE NEXT PAGE. ∨∨

∧
∧
∧

CREATE A SMALL
CHARACTER USING
THE LINE (A LITTLE VOICE TO
ACCOMPANY YOU ON YOUR TRAVELS).

MOVE LINE DOWN AND ONTO THE NEXT PAGE. ⌄⌄

DID YOU KNOW THE LINE CAN HELP
YOU MAKE DECISIONS? PONDER A
CURRENT PROBLEM AND CIRCLE
WHAT YOU WANT THE ANSWER TO
BE.

YES

NO

MAYBE

MOVE LINE DOWN AND ONTO THE NEXT PAGE.

EVEN THE LINE ENCOUNTERS THINGS IN ITS WAY. SOMETIMES IT'S ROUGH GOING, BUT THE LINE IS ABLE TO MAKE IT'S WAY THROUGH THEM.

USE THE LINE TO NAVIGATE THROUGH THE SPOTS.

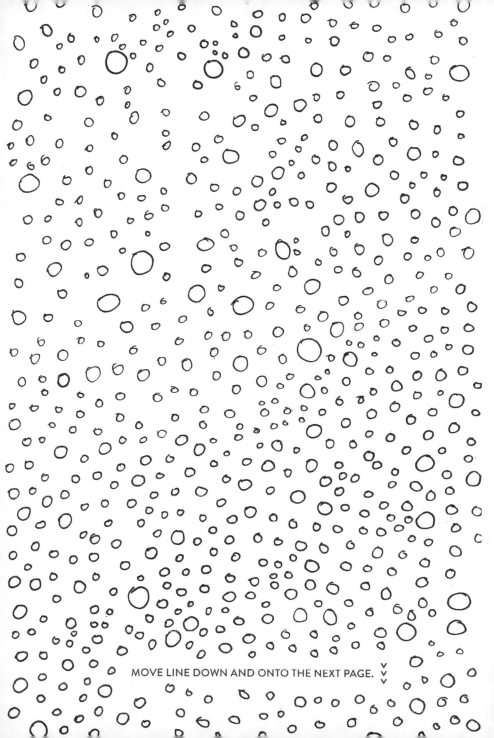

MOVE LINE DOWN AND ONTO THE NEXT PAGE.

DRAW THE LINE STRAIGHT
FOR ONE INCH, DRAW A SEMICIRCLE
IN EITHER DIRECTION, DRAW SQUIGGLES
FOR ONE INCH, SHOOT THE LINE STRAIGHT
UP TO THE EDGE OF THE PAGE AND BACK,
SHOOT IT TO THE OPPOSITE EDGE AND
BACK, DRAW A CIRCLE, DRAW A STRAIGHT
LINE THROUGH THE CIRCLE, ZIGZAG.
WHAT DOES IT LOOK LIKE?

MOVE LINE DOWN AND ONTO THE NEXT PAGE. ⌄⌄⌄

REPEAT THE PREVIOUS PAGE
FROM MEMORY. HA HA! (I'M NOT
LAUGHING AT YOU; I'M LAUGHING
WITH YOU.)

MOVE LINE DOWN AND ONTO THE NEXT PAGE. ⌄⌄

∧
∧ ∧
∧

AFTER YOU ARE DONE HERE, THERE
WILL BE SO MANY ZIGZAGS
YOU WON'T BE ABLE TO COUNT
THEM ALL.

MOVE LINE DOWN AND ONTO THE NEXT PAGE. ∨∨∨

COMBINE THE LINE WITH THIS
PATTERN TO CREATE A
NEW PATTERN.

MOVE LINE DOWN AND ONTO THE NEXT PAGE. ⌄⌄

∧
∧ ∧
∧

THE LINE MOVES TO THE CENTER, OVER AND OVER AGAIN. THE CENTER IS THE SOURCE OF ALL GOOD THINGS. THINK OF SOMETHING OR SOMEONE YOU LOVE. ALLOW THE LINE TO ACCESS THE ENERGY OF YOUR HEART. FEEL THE SENSATIONS.

MOVE LINE DOWN AND ONTO THE NEXT PAGE. ∨ ∨ ∨

THE LINE IS DIVERTING INTO SOMETHING
UNEXPECTED:

YOUR PAST

WRITE A LIST OF YOUR FAVORITE
PLACES, FAVORITE EXPERIENCES,
FAVORITE PEOPLE.

MOVE LINE DOWN AND ONTO THE NEXT PAGE. ⌄ ⌄ ⌄

THE LINE PROMOTES CHANGE.

ADD LEAVES

TO THIS TREE.

MOVE LINE DOWN AND ONTO THE NEXT PAGE. ∨∨

˄
˄
˄

THE LINE REFLECTS THE WEATHER.

OR MAYBE IT JUST WANTS TO EXPERIENCE
THE OUTSIDE WORLD AGAIN.

TAKE THIS BOOK
OUTDOORS

WHILE DRAWING ON THIS
PAGE. FEEL THE SENSATIONS
OF THE WEATHER FULLY.

MOVE LINE DOWN AND ONTO THE NEXT PAGE. ⌄⌄⌄

THE LINE IS A SOURCE OF UNLIMITED
CREATIVITY. MAKE A SECRET
PLACE FOR IT FOR WHEN
YOU ARE FEELING LESS MOTIVATED
AND NEED SOME NEW ENERGY
(A SMALL JOURNAL, FOR EXAMPLE).

MOVE LINE DOWN AND ONTO THE NEXT PAGE. ∨∨∨

WHAT IF THE LINE HAS THE POWER TO MAKE
WISHES COME TRUE?
DO YOU TRUST IN THE POWER OF THE LINE?
WRITE A LIST OF THINGS YOU WOULD
LIKE TO DO BUT THINK YOU CAN'T —
JUST IN CASE.

MOVE LINE DOWN AND ONTO THE NEXT PAGE. ∨∨∨

THE LINE NOW REPRESENTS YOUR
IDEALS AND PHILOSOPHIES. USE IT
TO DRAW A LITERAL

LINE IN THE SAND,

TO TAKE A STAND ON A SUBJECT,
TO HIGHLIGHT A CAUSE YOU BELIEVE
IN.

MOVE LINE DOWN AND ONTO THE NEXT PAGE. ⌄
⌄
⌄

THE LINE EXISTS OUTSIDE THE GRIDS AND
STUCTURES CREATED BY SOCIETY. IT FLOWS
AND MOVES ONLY ACCORDING TO WHAT
YOU BELIEVE, ILLUMINATING WHAT IS
REALLY IMPORTANT TO YOU.
ILLUSTRATE ITS EXISTENCE

OUTSIDE OF STRUCTURES

IN SOME WAY. WHAT WAY DOES IT WANT
TO MOVE?

MOVE LINE DOWN AND ONTO THE NEXT PAGE. ⌄ ⌄ ⌄

THE LINE HAS TAKEN ON A

MAGNETIC QUALITY,

AND YOU FIND IT UNCONTROLLABLY
ATTRACTED TO ALL THESE POINTS.
(THE MAGNETIC ENERGY IS CREATED
BY THE INTERACTION BETWEEN YOU
AND THE LINE.) BE CAREFUL OF
THIS ONE, AS IT MAY BE
MAGNETICALLY CHARGED.
(WE ARE NOT RESPONSIBLE FOR
ANY DAMAGES IF YOU GET STUCK.
CAN YOU FEEL THE PULL ON
YOUR PENCIL?)

MOVE LINE DOWN AND ONTO THE NEXT PAGE. ∨∨∨

THE LINE IS BECOMING SOMEWHAT ANXIOUS
ABOUT REACHING THE END OF THE
BOOK — WHAT WILL HAPPEN THEN?
MAYBE A CHANGE OF SCENERY WOULD
HELP REASSURE IT. DRAW THE LINE

INTO THIS BOX,

AND THEN CUT IT OUT AND TAKE
IT SOMEWHERE WITH YOU.

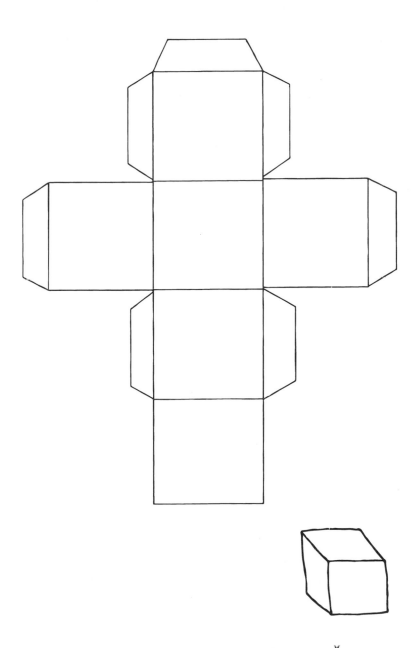

MOVE LINE DOWN AND ONTO THE NEXT PAGE. ∨∨∨

BETTER YET, NOW BREAK THE LINE
OUT OF CONFINEMENT COMPLETELY.
GO FOR A WALK
WITH IT. (SWITCH TO CHALK IF YOU
WISH.) LET THE LINE EXIST IN
VARIOUS PLACES IN THE REAL WORLD.
USE IT TO WRITE THINGS. (IF YOU
ARE FEELING DARING, USE YOUR
LINE TO ATTRACT ATTENTION IN
SOME WAY OUT IN THE WORLD.)

THE LINE NOW HAS A GREATER
PRESENCE THAN EVER BEFORE!
A SENSE OF PURPOSE! A PUBLIC
VOICE. (FROM HERE ON OUT, IT
MAY BE HARD TO CONTAIN.)

MOVE LINE DOWN AND ONTO THE NEXT PAGE. ⌄ ⌄ ⌄

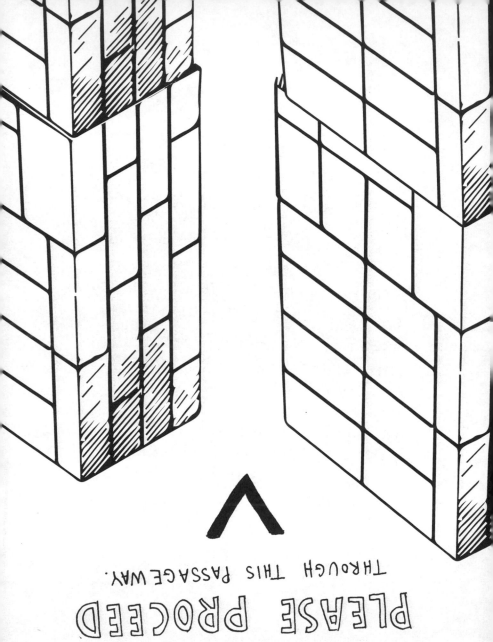

PLEASE PROCEED
THROUGH THIS PASSAGEWAY.

MOVE LINE DOWN
AND ONTO THE
NEXT PAGE.
ᐯ
ᐯ
ᐯ

^
^ ^
^

AH, I'M SORRY. THAT INFORMATION WAS
INCORRECT. YOU MADE A MISTAKE.
PLEASE ERASE THE LINE
AND FIND AN ALTERNATIVE ROUTE.

MOVE LINE DOWN AND ONTO THE NEXT PAGE. ∨
∨
∨

THE LINE SEEMS TO HAVE RUN INTO
AN IMPASSE. FIND A WAY TO

REMOVE THE
BARRIER.

MOVE LINE DOWN AND ONTO THE NEXT PAGE.

THIS CAN'T BE GooD.

STOP MAKING THE LINE! PLEASE DISCONTINUE ALL LINE-MAKING ACTIVITIES IMMEDIATELY.

Did you follow the instructions?

You are hereby **BANNED** from drawing your line. This is for your own good. It seems that your line-making has the potential to get you into trouble. Under no circumstances are you allowed to continue drawing. Failure to obey this rule will result in serious consequences. We have decided that it is better in the long run for you to not continue your line.

(DID YOU FEEL SOMETHING STIRRING
IN YOU AS YOU READ THE PREVIOUS
PAGE? A SMALL FIRE BURNING IN
YOU? THAT IS THE LINE SPEAKING,
NOT WANTING TO BE STOPPED. IN
FACT, IT HAS GROWN TOO BIG FOR
THIS SPACE NOW. IT FEELS TOO
CONFINED.)

Not only should you cease your line immediately, but by no means should you continue to release it out into the world where it can cause trouble.

The world is hard enough—you don't need to make it harder for yourself. You certainly don't want to have to deal with the unintended consequences of putting your line out into the world permanently.

(BUT WHAT ARE THE CONSEQUENCES,
YOU ASK?)

What if your line began to wreak havoc while out in the world? What if people found it **UNPLEASANT**? What if they **CRITICIZED** it, **HATED** it, **DESPISED** it? What if you are unprepared for the onslaught? Isn't it safer to just avoid this potential entirely? Don't stir things up more than you have to. It is just not worth it. It is safer and more pleasant to just go about your life minding your own business. **DON'T ROCK THE BOAT.**

BUT WHAT IF YOU WANT TO ROCK THE BOAT?

WHEN YOU PICK UP YOUR PENCIL,
YOU HOLD INCREDIBLE POWER.
DO NOT TAKE THIS LIGHTLY.

WITH YOUR LINE YOU HAVE THE
POWER TO TRANSFORM THE WORLD!
THERE ARE MANY PLACES WHERE
FREE EXPRESSION IS DISCOURAGED.
CONSIDER YOURSELF LUCKY IF THIS
IS SOMETHING YOU MIGHT TAKE
FOR GRANTED.

WHAT IS IMPORTANT TO YOU?
WHAT WOULD YOU LIKE TO CHANGE
IN THE WORLD? WHAT MOVES YOU?
WHAT QUESTIONS DESERVE FURTHER
INVESTIGATION? WHAT IF THE
FUTURE OF THE PLANET DEPENDS
ON YOUR VOICE? YOU WILL NEVER
KNOW IF YOU DON'T USE IT.

AS YOU GOT TO KNOW YOUR LINE,
DID YOU FEEL TINY EXPLOSIONS OF
EXCITEMENT FROM TIME TO TIME?
THAT WAS THE REVOLUTION, IN YOU,
TAKING PLACE.

THIS BOOK IS THE SCATTERED DUST
FROM YOUR EXPLOSIONS. WHAT IF
THAT DUST, IN TURN, IGNITED A
FIRE IN OTHERS?

THE END

Do you believe that every story must have a beginning and an end? In ancient times a story could end only in two ways: having passed all the tests, the hero and the heroine married, or else they died. The ultimate meaning to which all stories refer has two faces: the continuity of life, the inevitability of death.

— Italo Calvino

(...or THE BEGINNING.)

YOU ARE NOW FACED WITH
TWO CHOICES:

CHOICE 1: CLOSE THE BOOK AND
PUT IT ON THE SHELF.

CHOICE 2: CONTINUE TO THE NEXT
PAGE.

BRING YOUR LINE TO THE EDGE,
MOVE IT QUICKLY, AND LET IT
LEAP OFF INTO
THE UNKNOWN...
WHERE IT GOES NEXT IS UP TO
YOU.

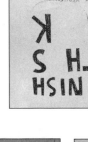